Golden Rules

Published by Willow Creek Press, P.O. Box 147, Minocqua,
Wisconsin 54548

Compiled and edited by Andrea Donner
Design by Patricia Bickner Linder

For information on other Willow Creek Press titles, call
850-9453

Library of Congress Cataloging-in-Publication Data

Bryan, Denver.
  Golden rules : virtues of the canine character / photographs
by Denver Bryan.
    p. cm.
  ISBN 1-57223-510-1 (hardcover : alk. paper)
  1. Golden retriever–Pictorial works. 2. Photography of dogs.
3. Quotations, English.
I. Title.
  SF429.G63 B78 200
    636.752'7–dc21
  2002003723

Printed in Canada

Golden Rules

Virtues of the Canine Character

Photographs by Denver Bryan

Willow Creek® PRESS

Accomplished

*Everyone enjoys doing the kind of work
for which he is best suited.*

NAPOLEON HILL

Happiness...it lies in the joy of achievement.

FRANKLIN DELANO ROOSEVELT

The highest of distinctions is service to others.

KING GEORGE VI

Clownish

Dogs laugh, but they laugh with their tails.

MAX FORRESTER EASTMAN

The great thing about a dog is that you may make a fool of yourself with him and not only will he not scold you, but he will make a fool of himself too.

SAMUEL BUTLER

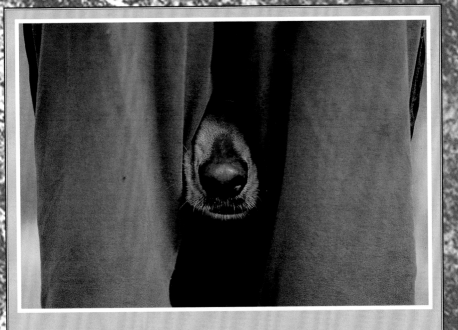

Like a welcome summer rain, humor may suddenly cleanse and cool the earth, the air and you.

LANGSTON HUGHES

Commitment

It seems essential, in relationships and all tasks,
that we concentrate only on what is most
significant and important.

SOREN KIERKEGAARD

A total commitment is paramount to reaching the ultimate in performance.

TOM FLORES

The achievement of your goal is assured the moment you commit yourself to it.

GEN. GEORGE S. PATTON

Determination

*Nothing in the world can
take the place of persistence . . . Persistence and
determination are omnipotent.*

ATTRIBUTED TO CALVIN COOLIDGE

He is able who thinks he is able.

BUDDHA

Energy and persistence conquer all things.

BENJAMIN FRANKLIN

Companions

A friend may well be reckoned the
masterpiece of nature.

RALPH WALDO EMERSON

Friends are treasures.

HORACE BRUNS

A faithful friend is the medicine of life.

ECCLESIASTICUS 6:16

Stay is a charming word in a friend's vocabulary.

LOUISA MAY ALCOTT

No one appreciates the very special genius of your conversation as much as the dog does.

CHRISTOPHER MORLEY

Affectionate

*When most of us talk to our dogs,
we tend to forget they're not people.*

JULIA GLASS

Who, being loved, is poor?

OSCAR WILDE

Our happiness in this world depends on the affections we are able to inspire.

DUCHESS PRAZLIN

Contentment

*Rest is not idleness, and to lie sometimes on the grass
on a summer day listening to the murmur of water,
or watching the clouds float across the sky,
is hardly a waste of time.*

Sir J. Lubbock

We never reflect how pleasant it is to ask for nothing.

SENECA

You can destroy your now worrying about tomorrow.

JANIS JOPLIN

He who does not care for Heaven but is contented where he is, is already in Heaven.

H.P. BLAVATSKY

The art of being happy lies in the power of extracting
happiness from common things.

HENRY WARD BEECHER

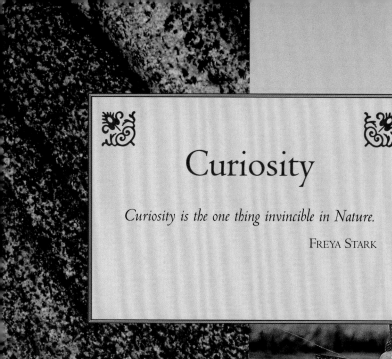

Curiosity

Curiosity is the one thing invincible in Nature.

FREYA STARK

Curiosity will conquer fear even more than bravery will.

JAMES STEPHENS

. . . *curiosity can be vivid and wholesome only in proportion as the mind is contented and happy.*

ANATOLE FRANCE

Desire

Clear your mind of can't.

SAMUEL JOHNSON

The starting point of all achievement is desire.

Napoleon Hill

Live that thou mayest desire to live again.

FRIEDRICH WILHELM NIETZSHE

Devotion

If you are not too long,
I will wait here for you all my life.

OSCAR WILDE

A real friend is one who walks in when the rest of the
world walks out.

WALTER WINCHELL

Dogs have given us their absolute all. We are the center of their universe, we are the focus of their love and faith and trust. They serve us in return for scraps. It is without a doubt the best deal man has ever made.

ROGER CARAS

A dog is the only thing on earth that loves you more than he loves himself.

JOSH BILLINGS

To his dog, every man is Napoleon, hence the constant popularity of dogs.

ALDOUS HUXLEY

Friendly

*There is no psychiatrist in the world
like a puppy licking your face.*

Ben Williams

The average dog is a nicer person than the average person.

ANDY ROONEY

Always hold your head up, but be careful to keep your nose at a friendly level.

MAX L. FORMAN

The greatest sweetener in life is friendship.

JOSEPH ADDISON

In order to really enjoy a dog, one doesn't merely try to train him to be semihuman. The point of it is to open oneself to the possibility of becoming partly a dog.

EDWARD HOAGLAND

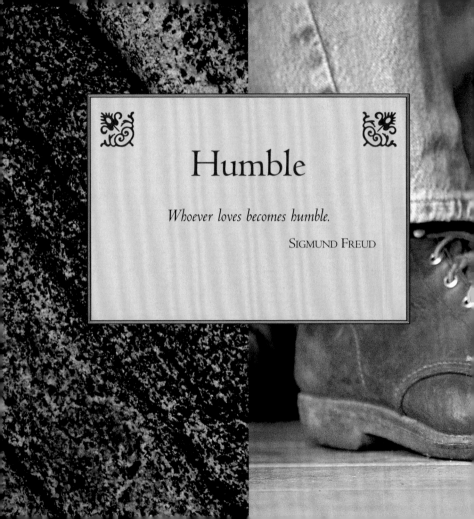

Humble

Whoever loves becomes humble.

SIGMUND FREUD

True humility is contentment.

HENRI FREDERIC AMIEL

Real excellence and humility are not incompatible one with the other, on the contrary they are twin sisters.

JEAN BAPTISTE LACORDAIRE

Intelligence

The dog has an enviable mind. It remembers the nice things in life and quickly blots out the nasty.

BARBARA WOODHOUSE

Life is a festival only to the wise.

RALPH WALDO EMERSON

The charming relations I have had with a long succession of dogs result from their happy spontaneity. Usually they are quick to discover that I cannot see or hear. Truly, as companions, friends, equals in opportunities of self-expression, they unfold to me the dignity of creation.

HELEN KELLER

Playful

Against the assault of laughter
nothing can stand.

MARK TWAIN

Follow your bliss.

Joseph Campbell

The time you enjoy wasting is not wasted time.

BERTRAND RUSSELL

The dog was created especially for children. He is the God of frolic.

HENRY WARD BEECHER

Joyful

*Good humor is one of the best articles of dress
one can wear in society.*

WILLIAM MAKEPEACE THACKERAY

All who would win joy, must share it;
happiness was born a twin.

LORD BYRON

Sometimes your joy is the source of your smile, but sometimes your smile can be the source of your joy.

THICH NHAT HANH

We know nothing of tomorrow; our business is to be good and happy today.

SYDNEY SMITH

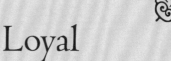

Loyal

The best things in life are never rationed.
Friendship, loyalty, love, do not require coupons.

G.T. HEWITT

There is no faith which has never yet been broken, except that of a truly faithful dog.

KONRAD LORENZ

Histories are more full of examples of the fidelity of dogs than of friends.

ALEXANDER POPE

Patience

Patience is the key to contentment.

MOHAMMED

The greatest power is often simple patience.

E. Joseph Cossman

Patience is the companion of wisdom.

SAINT AUGUSTINE

Potential

Joy comes from using your potential.

WILL SCHULTZ

Great ability develops and reveals itself increasingly with every new assignment.

BALTHASAR GRACIAN

Let him who would enjoy a good future waste none of his present.

ROGER BABSON

Trusting

The best proof of love is trust.

DR. JOYCE BROTHERS

You may be deceived if you trust too much, but you will live in torment if you don't trust enough.

FRANK CRANE

Enthusiasm

Zeal will do more than knowledge.

WILLIAM HAZLITT

Enthusiasm moves the world.

ARTHUR JAMES BALFOUR

You will do foolish things, but do them with enthusiasm.

COLETTE

*And in the end it's not the years in your life that count. It's
the life in your years.*

ABRAHAM LINCOLN